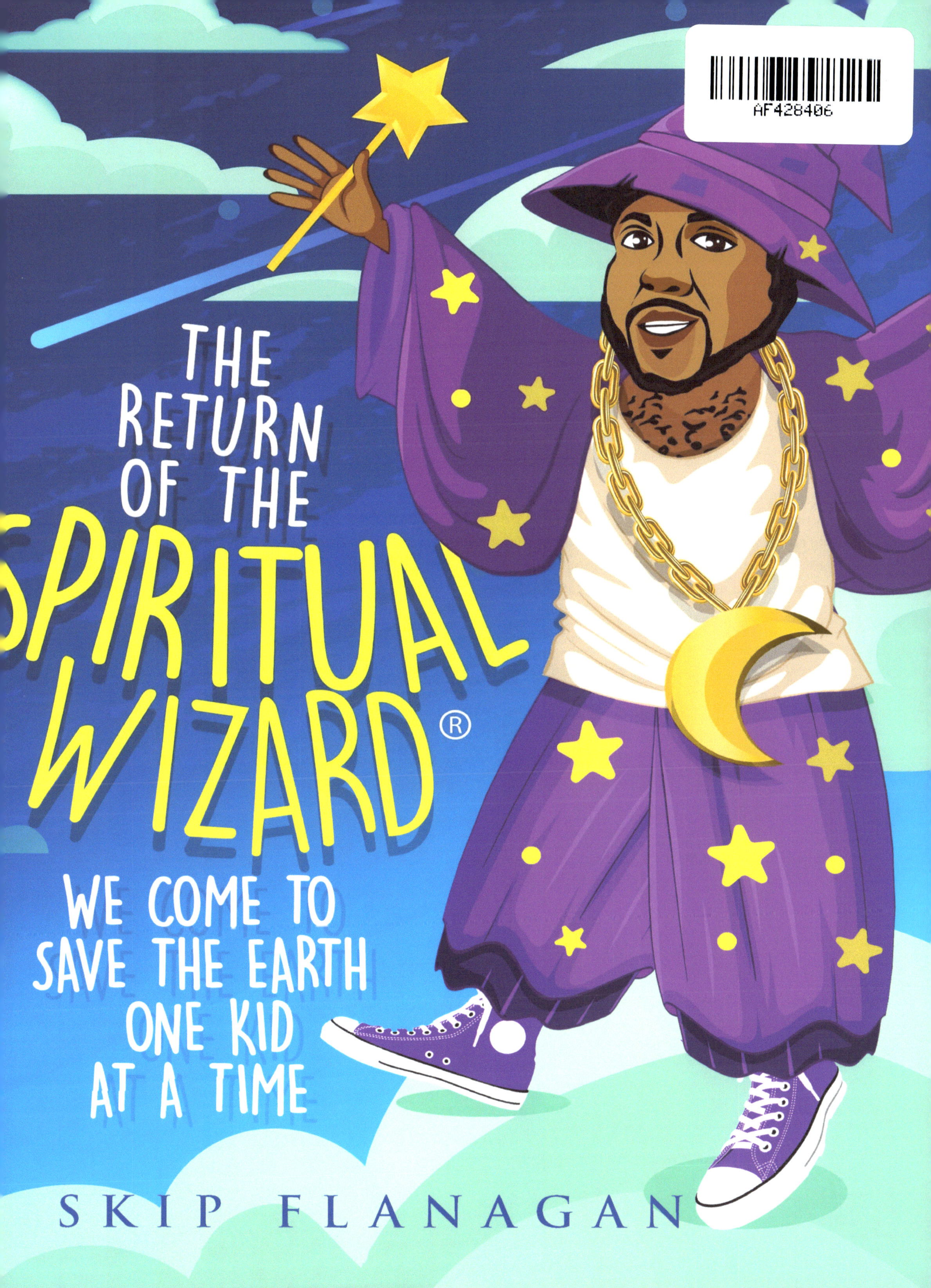

AF428406
THE RETURN OF THE SPIRITUAL WIZARD®
WE COME TO SAVE THE EARTH ONE KID AT A TIME
SKIP FLANAGAN

Library of Congress Control Number: 2024908724

ISBN: 979-8-89228-138-6   (Paperback)
ISBN: 979-8-89228-139-3   (eBook)

Printed in the United States of America

Lil Jason was a cool kid that loved sports. He loved music also. Lil Jason would take his cell phone to school even though his parents told him not to.

Lil Jason was in class. He pulls out his phone. Johnny the Bully asks Jason to use his phone. Lil Jason pulls out his phone again. Johnny then quickly grabs Lil Jason's phone. Lil Jason is upset and refuses to let his phone go. Finally, Johnny the bully was able to take Lil Jason's phone.

Lil Jason was upset. He ran home crying. Lil Jason was screaming to himself, "I'm going to hurt him!"

Tears we're running down Lil Jason's face. He was upset at the fact that his cellphone had been taken by the bully Johnny. Lil Jason always listens to rap music. His favorite song talked about hurting people. His favorite rapper was Bad Boy Mike. His favorite song was "Hurt them".

Lil Jason hurries and goes upstairs. He is scared because he knows he wasn't supposed to take his cellphone to school. His Mom and dad always told him not to take it to school. Lil Jason knew in his heart that he was in trouble. So, he decided to go straight to his room.
Lil Jason is in his room. He puts his bags down. He turns off the light. He is crying. Lil Jason is screaming," I'm going to hurt

Johnny! I promise I'm going to hurt him!" Lil Jason then grabs his baseball bat. Then he repeats, "I'm going to hurt him just wait and see!"
He beats on the floor. While beating on the floor he looks towards the mirror on the wall and a light comes on. The light

then goes away. So, he beats on the floor again. The light flickers again then disappears. So, he beats harder and faster. Then a wizard appears.

Lil Jason looks in the mirror. He is surprised. He sees a wizard. Then asks the wizard," Who are you?" The wizard then replies," I'm the spiritual wizard! My job is to help kids that are

having problems." Lil Jason replies, "I have a big problem do you think you can help me with it" The Wizard replies, "No problem is too big for the wizard except?" Lil Jason replies, "What do you mean except?" the Wizard replies, "I heard you say you were. going to hurt someone. I can't help you if you hurt people. My job is to help people that have been hurt by other people." Lil Jason replies "Rapper Bad Boy Mike says you have to hurt people that take your stuff." Lil Jason then asks the wizard, "Do you know rapper bad boy Mike?"

The wizard replies, "I do not know rapper Mike, but you need to choose better rappers to listen to." I listen to Skip Flanagan. He has good music. Lil Jason smiles and replies, "You are old school that's why you like Skip Flanagan." The wizard replies, "I guess you can say that. I just like good music." The wizard continues. "The only way I can help you is if you promise not to hurt the guy that took your phone and you go and tell your teacher to get it back for you. Can you do that?" Lil Jason replies, "But I wasn't supposed to have my phone at school. My Mom is going to whoop me and I'm going to get in trouble at school." The wizard replies, "When we don't follow instructions this is what happens. Sometimes we must accept the penalties for our actions." The wizard continues "Can you go and tell your teacher about your problem? She"

can help you and I will help you." Lil Jason replies, "Yes I will do it but I'm going to get in trouble." The Wizard explains, "I promise I will help you. Do you trust me?" Lil Jason replies "Yes. I will do it" The wizard replies "OK." Lil Jason is sad and scared. He knows that he was not supposed to take his cell phone to school. His mom and dad have told him lots of times not to take his cellphone to school. But Lil Jason never listens. Now Johnny the bully has the phone, and he can't get it back. The Wizard speaks again. "I need you to do a couple of things for me." I need you to memorize these words. It goes like this, Father God help me to be a better kid. Father God help me to obey my parents. Father God teach me how to be kind to others and never hurt anyone. Amen. After you go to your teacher and tell her your problem. Come back and knock on the floor 4 times. When you knock 4 times I will appear. Make sure the room is dark and you are alone. Can you do that?" Lil Jason replies, "Yes Sir!" The wizard replies, "I knew you were a good kid."

Lil Jason gets on his knees. He recites the prayer that the wizard gave him over and over until he remembers it. He thinks about the things that the wizard said. He makes a promise to himself that he will change and be a better kid.

Lil Jason then goes to sleep and gets ready for the next day.

Lil Jason gets on the bus and heads to school. He is feeling a little better because of his talk with the wizard. Lil Jason really likes the wizard. No one has ever tried to talk to him or help him. I guess this means that rapper Bad Boy Mike is his new enemy. Lil Jason now understands that rapper Bad Boy Mike has been giving him bad information.

Lil Jason arrives at school. He walks down the hallway. He sees Johnny the bully. He looks and walks past him. Lil Jason walks into classroom early before the class begins. He wants to talk to the teacher before the other kids get into the classroom. He is afraid they will call him a snitch. He tells the teacher what happened. The teacher says, "I'm sorry that happened to you. But you know you were not supposed to have your phone at school?" Lil Jason replies "Yes Mam" The teacher looks at Lil Jason and says "Wow you seem like you are a little different. Your parents must have disciplined you?" Lil Jason replies "No. They don't know. I talked to the wizard." The teacher smiles. Then she replies, "Okay wizard! You go ahead and go back outside, and I'll take care of this Mr. Wizard." And then she smiles.

Lil Jason goes back outside. He is playing with the school kids. The bell rings. It's time to go to class. Lil Jason goes to class. Johnny the bully is in class. The teacher begins teaching. Johnny the bully pulls out the cellphone he took from Lil Jason. The teacher sees the cellphone and walks over to Johnny the bully. She asks "Johnny give me that phone you know you are not supposed to have that phone at school" Johnny the Bully gives her the phone. Johnny the Bully then explains "It's not my phone. It belongs to Lil Jason. "The teacher asks, "If the phone belongs to Jason what are you doing with it?" Johnny the bully replies "Jason let me use it" Lil Jason responds, "I didn't let him use my phone he took my phone!" The teacher then responds, "Be quiet Lil Jason I will handle this!" Lil Jason sits back in his chair. He is upset.

The teacher takes the phone from Johnny the bully. Lil Jason is smiling now. A few minutes later the class ends. The teacher instructs Lil Jason to come to her desk. She begins to explain to him that he should never bring his cellphone to school. She says, "I'm going to call your mother and have her come and pick up the phone." Lil Jason is afraid now because his mother told him not to bring his cellphone to school. The teacher continues "I know it's not what you wanted but when you make mistakes you must pay for them." She then asks, "Do you understand?" Lil Jason replies, "Yes Mam" She continues, "I want you to join the school basketball team. It will be good for you. You will learn about teamwork and sportsmanship. Go to Coach Jiles room and tell him I sent you there," Lil Jason smiles then he replies "Ok. Thanks for getting my phone back."
The teacher responds "No problem. Just don't bring it back to school" Lil Jason replies "I won't. I learned my lesson"

Lil Jason is excited. He turns and runs home. His mom is on her way to school to pick up his cellphone. Lil Jason talked to Coach Jiles. Coach Jiles told him to come to basketball practice tomorrow. Lil Jason was on the basketball team. Lil Jason is happy! Lil Jason has learned a valuable lesson. Now he is excited and wants to share the good news with the wizard.

The wizard looks at Lil Jason. Lil Jason looks at the wizard. Lil Jason asks, "Why didn't you answer. I was knocking and you didn't answer?" The wizard explains, "It sounded like a bunch of noise. I gave you instructions. You must learn to follow instructions. That is the moral of the story. You must follow instructions. Notice how when you follow instructions everything turns out right?" Lil Jason replies "Yes Sir!" The wizard responds, "I will only appear when you follow instructions. Make sure you are alone. Make sure it's dark in your room. Make sure you knock 4 times. Do you understand?" Lil Jason replies "Yes Sir!"

The wizard then asks, "How are you doing?" Lil Jason is excited. He explains, "I have some good news!" The wizard then asks, "What news is that?" Lil Jason Continues, "I got my phone back!" The wizard answers, "That's great news! How did you get it back?" Lil Jason replies, "I asked my teacher for help just like you told me to do. After I told her about my phone. She went and took my phone away from Johnny the bully." The wizard responds, "That's great news!" Lil Jason excitedly adds, "I also made the basketball team!" The wizard smiles, "That's great now one last thing which is the most important thing. Did you learn the prayer?" Lil Jason quickly responds, "Yes! Yes! I learned it the first day!" The wizard is impressed at the fact that

Lil Jason has memorized the prayer. The wizard then asks, "Can you repeat the prayer?" Lil Jason replies "Yes Sir! I can repeat it!" The wizard says, "Let's hear it!" Lil Jason begins" Father God help me to be a better kid. Father God help me to obey my parents. Father God teach me how to be kind to others and never hurt anyone. Amen."
Lil Jason recites the prayer successfully. He then looks up to the wizard and smiles. The wizard smiles back. The wizard replies, "That was good. You did a good job. Now think about what would have happened if you had hurt your friend. You would be in a lot of trouble. "Lil Jason replies, I'm glad I listened to you Mr. Wizard. I wouldn't have been able to play basketball. I promise I will never hurt anyone. You must let grown ups manage tough situations until you are old enough to manage them yourself."

The wizard smiles. Then the wizard says, "You never want to hurt anyone. When you hurt people you don't get a second chance not to hurt them. You are a kid. You must learn to let grownups manage situations until you are old enough to manage them yourself. You also must learn how to follow instructions. That will be important in life and in sports. If you don't follow instructions; the coach can't teach you the plays. Always say the prayer in the morning when you wake up and when you are ready to go to sleep. Last, ask your parents to recite the Lord's Prayer to you and remember it as well. I'm leaving now. I will return whenever I see that you are having problems. If you need me always follow the instructions and I will appear. Wonderful job! Goodbye!"

The wizard disappears. Lil Jason looks and puts his head down. He picks up his basketball and runs outside and plays basketball on his basketball goal. Lil Jason is happy.